salmonpoetry

What Our Shoes Say About Us

GERARD HANBERRY

Published in 2014 by
Salmon Poetry
Cliffs of Moher, County Clare, Ireland
Website: www.salmonpoetry.com
Email: info@salmonpoetry.com

ISBN 978-1-908836-32-8

COVER IMAGE: © Lucie Lang | Dreamstime.com
COVER DESIGN & TYPESETTING: *Siobhán Hutson*
Printed in Ireland by Sprint Print

Salmon Poetry gratefully acknowledges the support of
The Arts Council / An Chomhairle Ealaoín

Acknowledgments

Acknowledgements are due to the editors of the following journals and newspapers in which some of these poems first appeared, a number of them in slightly different versions:

The Stinging Fly, The Irish Times, The Stony Thursday Book, Blue Max Review (Fermoy), *Revival, The Galway Review, Crannóg, The Galway Advertiser, The City Tribune, The Sunday Tribune, Mala* (The Chengdu Bookworm Literary Journal, China), *Grocott's Mail* (Grahamstown, South Africa), *Dogs Singing: A Tribute Anthology* (Salmon Poetry), *Watching My Hands at Work: A Festschrift for Professor Adrian Frazier* (Salmon Poetry).

Poems have also been broadcast on RTE Radio, Galway Bay FM, Midwest Radio, Phoenix FM, Victoria, Australia.

The poem "Embers" won the Brendan Kennelly Poetry Prize, held to mark the poet's retirement from Trinity College, Dublin and judged by Prof. Terrence Browne. First published in *The Sunday Tribune* the poem was subsequently published in a limited edition, hand-bound collection called *Something Like Lovers* from Stonebridge Publishing, Wales.

The poem "Crossing Eyre Square" won the Galway County and Galway City Council's Poetry Prize (2009) for a poem celebrating Eyre Square, Galway.

Contents

Make-Believe

It is 1964 and the wind is his playmate
as he walks tall on the stilts of five full years.

He is strangely aware of being happy today
in the sunshine with his plastic football, a birthday gift.

The goblins have withdrawn for the afternoon
and it is safe to leave the stockade,

to go into the fields alone
with a basket for blackberries,

to talk to strangers,
to cross the road

and for the first time ever
climb to the tip of the great chestnut,

stand high where the pennon would flap
if the tree was really a circus big-top

and gaze down on a pretend world
released from fear,

where Dads in smart shirts arrive home from work
driving shiny cars with big tailfins

having stopped by the *candy store*
like the Dads in the TV families

who smile at their children and kiss their wives,
saying happy words such as *honey* and *gee whizz*,

where the dog knows that it is safe
to bark and wag its tail.

Intervention

The afternoon smells of hot tar.
A car arrives at the gate
as if out of the blue.

She is in bed.
Anything could happen.
He is sitting in the porch

like a stranger on a park bench
staring at a frozen pond.
Nobody has bothered to pick up the shattered glass.

The driver walks up the path,
sees the boy under the hedge,
says 'Hello, big fellow!',

gives him money to go to the shop for ice-cream.
There is no shop, no ice-cream, so the boy
goes instead to the field at the end of the road,

sits on a warm stone for a long time watching a fly family
on their happy Sunday afternoon hike
across freshly plopped cow-poos.

Daddy fly has a long stick for poking the dung,
Mommy fly has a furry belly, the children wear tiny
fly-wellingtons, three pairs each for their six legs.

When the boy comes back
the walls of the house are no longer trembling,
someone has put fresh milk in the fridge.

Did She Ever Dance?

Did she ever dance,
light and spontaneous,
in her clinched youth
when all the rooms were dark
as the burdened sky or the lake?

And the grass was always dark
even on summer days
when the wild roses and bell-fuchsias
drooped along the hedgerows
down to the grey shore.

Did she ever hear laughter
in a house whose walls were grey,
like the flagstone floor
where she knelt every night,
stringing her faults like a rosary

all the way to her mother's grey eye,
and later unspooling to her husband's,
the heavy tablecloth and dinner service,
the dark hall, the stairs, the room,
the ticking of a grandfather clock.

Monsters of Earthly Delights

They told us we were born sinners
destined to burn for all eternity
in the roaring flames of Hell.

We learned their Catechism by rote,
they beat us with sticks
when we faltered.

There were seven sins, they said,
more deadly than all the rest,
monsters of earthly delights

but look at them now,
shrivelled creatures in a forgotten zoo,
a freak-show

saved from extinction
but condemned
to gaze listlessly

on the young strollers
who wander in to mock
this curious menagerie of vices,

fed, watered, made comfortable
by a few fervent devotees,
one of whom, it is rumoured,

comes alone at night,
enters the cages naked,
pleading with the beasts to arise,

rip his flesh to pieces,
to at least snap his right hand
off at the wrist.

The Great Puzzler

On the third day
we found him,
stiff and stretched
by the side of the back lane,
white fur muddied,
blood clotted behind his ear.

Tears in the kitchen, the keen probings
of an anguished nine-year-old.
We satisfied her how,
her where, her when?
But then the great puzzler,
the impossible 'why'?

Ringo

Dad said he had the look of a Teddy Boy
and should be sent back to the Home.
Mom said he was like one of 'The Beatles'

with his shaggy black coat and tumbling fringe.
Get Back reached number one that week
so we called him Ringo Starr.

I knew straight off that his rock n' roll sneer
was a shield, his swagger a defence against the street.
He settled right in and was mine.

Ringo knew the score and probably chewed gum
out back of his kennel while he waited
for the neighbourhood to heat up.

I could tell he knew a lot more than me about girls.
An astronaut stepped onto the Sea of Tranquillity
and someone was singing about the year 2525.

Dad was at home a lot that long winter,
spent weeks hammering in the shed.
Mom went off to a job somewhere every day.

I could hear them talking at night. They sounded cross.
Ringo wanted to go exploring by moonlight
so we sneaked off.

Spring and Dad had work once again.
A girl smiled and said hello to me on the bus,
I thought about her all week.

Friday and Ringo's bowl lay untouched.
That night he failed to make it home.
We worried but he did have a wild streak.

We searched, Dad, myself, a neighbour.
Nothing. For two nights his kennel stood empty.
A farmer checking cattle saw the black bundle,

drugs in the system with a hint of foul play,
a fitting end given his rock-star style.
We carried him home. Mom planted a shrub and it grew.

1.   First Dance

Youthawkward, with the cut of a blackguard,
a patched-beggar in a psychedelic shirt,
arriving at your side
tongue in a hangman's knot,

the first dance a tumble of lurchings
and foot-buckling highland flings.
You fled but circled.
Cornered later for the slow set,

I had you where I wanted you now,
pinned close and in my element.
You stood your ground, checked my stealth,
then the faintest of finger-tightenings,

feather-light but enough to be going on with,
slow-dancing in a room with no windows.
Was it then you glimpsed how it could be,
my skittering heart no longer my own?

Familiar bearings scooped from under our feet
and flung towards the moon.

2. On Nimmo's Pier

The shy knock of the Claddaghmen's boats,
the current easy, the tide full in.

Long Walk and the stars mingling
on the river's lustrous face,

the world turned upside down,
our lips tingling for more.

At the pier's curved limit
great cubes of limestone offer shelter.

The summer breeze skin-salty,
the Corrib's mouth wide open.

The lighthouse blinks its warning
over the deep breath-heavings of the sea.

3.   Undercut

There we were on the Aran ferry
out from Galway docks,

churning through diesel fumes and sunshine between
the Burren's familiar blue hills and the low coast road,

the place strangely transformed, like a dream-country,
we had never been on the Bay before.

At the cliffs we bellied across great fissured slabs
to the open yawn of sky and sea, felt the giddy tug,

gulls and light cartwheeling,
the swell hunching far below.

Huge stone shelves undercut and all about
the evidence of sudden collapse.

I felt you shudder, a cloud veiled the sun.
We can't depend on it, you whispered.

Your hand squeezed mine,
I drew you back, crab-crawling.

We kissed, I remember,
but it was a long time before you spoke.

Painting the Bedroom

Freshly painted in 'Moonlight Blue'
to capture the light or so it says on the tin.

Outside, the silent star-language of time,
seasons swinging by in buds and blossoms.

Let us wrap this room around us, lover,
kneading infinity into every pore of our desire,

grasping it tightly
between the palms of our hands.

First Skirmish

Brief but enough,
gatling cacophony,

rapid-fire gutturals
strafing the kitchen floor.

No prisoners, no mercy,
an orderly retreat,

the stairs and landing mined.
Smoking arrows thrum

where they lodged
in the living-room wall.

Now he glares at the travel channel,
the remote a pocket-pistol,

she's on the couch
trawling Facebook for sympathy,

the flag on the high ground
limp and in tatters.

Shades

Yesterday I was the bending fish
trapped in the tiny swirlpool by the humpback bridge
and you were the river's gentle current
stroking the smooth pebbles on the sandy bed.

Later, you were the yellow light between the curtains
in the third-floor window and I was the man
in the long coat and hat with a cigarette
leaning against the streetlamp down below.

This morning, I admit that you were right all along,
being the gentle current,
therefore I am no longer the bending fish
in the dark pool.

Instead, I am now the silent heron
standing upstream among the reeds,
dressed in a grey cloak and sporting dark shades
very like the expensive pair you brought home from Italy,

the ones I wear only on state occasions
or that one time in the privacy
of our fancy hotel room in Cascais
at two o'clock in the morning.

Garden Path

Imagine lover
what it would have been like

had we managed
to slip past that dozy guard

at the rose-garden gate
that night when we had the chance.

Instead, we settled
for artificial flowers,

this chemical whiff,
and worse —

we got used to it,
eventually.

Embers

When Apollo ordered Mithras to sacrifice a bull
he carried out the task unwillingly, mosaics depict
his face averted. As the bull died the animal became
the moon, Mithras' mantle the starry sky.

From the bull's blood the first corn sprouted,
the first purple grapes. Every other thing sprang
from his seed, except the scorpion.
The scorpion drinks seed and blood.

*

Their days are passed in silences
or set pieces, coming and going,
holding out as best they can,
retreating into props and costumes
and south facing rooms,
ignoring the fact that no one ever calls.

And still they make love,
more in hope than passion,
like two castaways
keeping the signal-fire burning
on the off chance,
taking turns to fan the embers,

to straighten the help sign
built with white stones
along their beach.
Each night the great breakers roll in
to wipe away the footprints,
now his, now hers.

*

The old cartographers were right;
it is possible to drop off the edge of the world
and monsters of the deep exist
exactly where the ancient charts placed them.

*

Spires of pine trees, medieval, here and there on the
    amber hillside;
silence not yet shattered by traffic on the Strada Aurelia.

She sleeps little in this high-ceilinged room, her fears
    rustling
like night-creatures in the wood, the air already dry as
    dead leaves.

Yesterday, a man in the gift-shop smiled but it was not
a stranger's smile she wanted. No, not his, not his.

A great bird, a hawk maybe, rises broad-winged and
    circles, circles,
white petals curl on the veranda, pearl-shells loose from
    the patterned wall.

On the bedside table near his sleeping head,
the door-sign in bold lettering – DO NOT DISTURB.

*

Where the ancient river winds
through the scorched earth of Campagna
it's hard to know east from west.
A lizard, throat pulsing in the heat,
clings to a rock, waits, listens,
then slithers for his dusty crevice.

She remains in the Piazza while he climbs
the stairs to the Basilica's great dome.

26

Higher, higher, slowly winding, a hymn, a chant,
perhaps it's not too late, my love, perhaps it's not too late.
Then the city spreads before him, the curving
colonnades of St. Peter's, elliptical, like a claw.

He sees her far below among the wandering tourists,
standing near the fountain, tiny, unmistakable.
He wants to call out. The sky is marble blue and
beautiful; they were right to come. But she moves,
crossing by Nero's obelisk, its shadow long and black
across the square, a tail, its sharp point the sting.

*

They have arrived at the ruins of Ostia.
He thumbs the guidebook in the shade,
cap pulled low against the blaze of white sunlight,
she prowls the edges, making her own way

through empty courtyards, the tilt and stagger
of columns, to the still of an amphitheatre where
she sits, knees drawn up, watching three wild cats
move away over the steps like wishes softly rebuffed.

In the cool of Mithras' Temple they share Casareccio
bread and Chianti, splashing wine into plastic cups,
red droplets falling on the mosaic floor, on the scorpion
and across the bull, his neck stretched for the blade.

By the Via Ostiense they sit apart in deepening shadow,
down this ancient road an Empire marched,
no clang of legions now, no throb of seed and blood,
just the dry crackle of their plastic cups.

Then faint through the ages and the gathering twilight,
drawn perhaps by their dismay, their defeat, come faded
sounds, a woman sobbing, a door being nailed and shuttered,
the last bundled cart creaking up the road for Rome.

Reading the Tome

It is the silence that eventually prompts me to halt.
No barrage of questions delivered in a small voice,

no tugging at the coat-tails or the usual endless queries
about the meaning of peculiar words.

I realise my mind has wandered off again
like a curious tourist evading the guide.

Nothing for it but to return to the point of separation,
to check at every junction

until the missing wits are located
probably down a narrow backstreet,

gazing at the skimpy outfits in the window
of a store called Fantasia,

not a stone's throw from the part of town
that only comes alive after dark.

Lost

He still finds her lips
in the shrouding mists off the bay,

her arms in the red July breeze
wrapping itself around his neck

when he shuffles
over Wolf Tone Bridge,

her body-sway in the wild tunes
leaping from the Quay Street bars,

her voice in every
side-alley whisper.

The stepping-stones to her lake-home
sunk in the quagmire of his folly,

in the gurgle of a life
swirling down the drain.

Tomorrow

He will wake once more
to the blank infinity

of another day.
Immense, glacial.

The sky vacant,
the horizon far off.

He will fall to his knees
like a beggar in a deserted village,

his scream will be silent
and more terrible for that.

Denial

Her substance fading
atom by atom

from the roots of her greying hair,
through cheek bones and neck sinews,

shoulders, breasts, waist, womb,
hollow and shadowless,

crumbling the length of her thighs,
shinbones, the balls of her feet

but still holding out,
incredulous,

nothing definite,
only a rummage of dust,

powdered like crushed glass
beneath her hobnailed denial.

(ii)

The leer of a hired-room mirror,
sunlight piercing between heavy drapes,

six-o'clock chimes, the lie
sticky on the soles of stockinged feet.

Ghosting through the white-tiled lobby,
their phones back on.

Still tingling, oh yes,
and gone completely to the dogs.

Truth Will Out

Stripped of polite disguises
no use for that now

dredged from the gut
slung with sawn-off force

blistering cacophony
bare-knuckled and to the bone.

Bordertime

When you come to me again
across bordertime

we will drive through country roads
in our lime-green Hillman Hunter

and sail through the eyes of stone bridges
to the sound of accordion music,

climb steps with the ease of shadows,
to gaze over lead-green domes,

wander deep into side-streets
where the market stalls are laden

with boxes of ripening mangoes
and tubs of shiny olives,

you in that floral swing-skirt,
me with a silly Panama.

The street sweepers
in their unbuttoned overalls

will bow to your loveliness
as we pass,

every corner we turn
teeming with sunlight and tomorrows.

(ii)

The cold truth is I don't often leave my room anymore
and the Matron tends to avoid me.

In fact I enjoy sitting by my window now,
remembering our dead friends,

sometimes I glimpse them out there among the trees.
I tell the nurses that my sons are delayed at the airport,

that my wife is off somewhere in a beautiful dress.
I let them think I believe these things.

Maybe some night when the moon is round and perfect
my wife will actually appear

walking up the drive towards my window
in her sky-blue dress

her dark hair glistening, yes,
her dark hair glistening in the moonlight.

(iii)

Do you recall that summer's evening
years ago up on Clifton Bridge,

petrified high-wire walkers,
Avon Gorge yawning below?

We were hoping to spot a falcon,
they were nesting on the cliffs above the river.

A great orange balloon sailed over,
basket swinging, pilot waving,

then another and another, reds, striped, golden,
until the sky filled with flying balloons.

Of course you remember,
I am not imagining,

and kissing, yes, kissing up there on the bridge,
our lives prancing young,

then the long stroll back to town
the falcon's nest forgotten.

Sakura

In Okinawa to the south
the first Sakura blooms.

The petal shower creeps slowly north
towards Kyote and Tokyo,

a gentle flower-wave,
tracked all the way by lovers

impatient for their own blossoming,
their Hanami kiss beneath the tree.

(Sakura is the beautiful Japanese Flowering
Cherry, symbol of love and rejuvenation. Hanami is
a traditional picnic beneath the blooming tree.)

Intrusion

The voice on the phone
wore a uniform:

No burglar alarm?
Foolish in this day and age.

I watch you walk the tumbled house
trying not to caress what had been pawed,

drawers hanging like the tongues of dead cattle,
the air smudged and quivering when we come in.

Everywhere, the crude smash and scatter,
their derisive laugh still echoing.

'Not a lot for them to take anyway,'
then you stop by the empty sideboard,

two vague circles like stamps on an old passport
where our porcelain figurines had poised for years,

wedding gifts,
intact in their elegant world,

the slender ballerina
stretching high on her tiptoes,

her kneeling partner
balanced for the clinch.

Hobson's Choice

Embrace the flame and the finality of ashes
wind-scattered from a pitching rib

or rest facing the rising sun
in one skeletal piece, skull to tarsals,

as if waiting for some final inspection
before the trumpet blast and the great awakening.

Says more about our lives as lived
than how we might wish to ride out eternity.

It's like having a favoured position for lovemaking
on Friday nights after the Late Show

while youth hops the cemetery wall down the road
with a bottle of Buckfast and a condom

to snatch a little pleasure from the flesh
in the shadows behind the yews.

What Our Shoes Say About Us

(i)

He spoke of 'clean dirt', 'honest sweat',
of always paying your own way in a world
forever pointing him towards the side entrance.

Shiny shoes were only for the Sabbath.
Six days of the week my father wore
the heavy boots of a working man.

They stood to attention inside the door,
ankle-leather kept supple
as elephant's ears,

ready for the morning:
*Mind your boots
and your boots will mind you.*

He held the one word with Polonious
when it came to lending and borrowing,
the returned emigrant's suspicion of drink

and the wish to see his own son wear
clean shirts and polished shoes
seven days of the week.

(ii)

Six policemen with Winchesters
shot a man in Utah last night,

fired a volley of bullets at a target
fixed to the prisoner's chest

as he sat hooded and strapped to a chair
in a room with white cinderblock walls.

The reporters did not mention
the convict's footwear.

Perhaps he walked barefooted
through the sandbags

to that high-backed throne on its little pedestal
facing the gunport slit,

flexing his toes
to catch the last curve of the earth,

heard the firing-squad troop in,
regulation footwear spit and polished for the occasion.

Later they would crunch across the gravel yard
to their cars, nod to each other,

ignoring the chanters at the gate.
'Honey, I'm home!'

    (iii)

Cardinal red, of the finest Morocco leather,
soft as warm cheese,

coloured with precious dye from molluscs
or the grindings of beetles' shells.

At one time gold braided and bucked
the better to receive the visitor's kiss,

walking metaphors of blood and martyrs,
the Pope's special footwear when out of doors,

fashioned today by the cobbler from Novara
for the feet of 'the fisher of men'.

(iv)

Blue, with suede uppers,
impeccable, inviolable,

Saturday night neon,
a cruising Cadillac,

boulevard waltzing,
rock, roll and shuffle,

look but do not touch,
so let's dance, honey,

let me jive you all the way
to my great Hall of Fame.

(v)

The world's oldest shoe has been found
in an Armenian cave, well preserved,
buried in sheep dung for over five thousand years.

The excited curator at Toronto's shoe museum
described a stylish moccasin,
cut from a single piece of cowhide,

laced along seams at the instep and heel,
tanned and tailor-made for the right foot,
the shoe of a rich man, so ancient yet so familiar.

She told the interviewer that,
going by the style of the antique loafer,
not a lot had changed in five millennia.

Finding Ink

Should any words of mine find ink today
they will take the shape of fugitives
loose from a fogbound prison-hulk

where they have languished half-imagined,
growing brutal and suspicious,
deprived so long of fancy's dreamy caress.

Guttural mumblings of resentment
is all you will hear as they
lumber in at feeding time,

banging their wooden bowels,
disturbing any casual observer
with their stubby deformities.

Creation

All those tadpole-thoughts
wriggling and squirming,

a jelly-sperm genesis
in the swampy undergrowth,

writhing towards daylight
to sit for an afternoon and croak

to a world rapt in its own
terrifying indifference.

Anthology Café

So this is where all the poems come
to eye each other up,
to snigger and bitch
over fancy cocktails,

mocking the jaded clichés
still loud and glitzy at the bar
or the pale metaphors with fraying cuffs
who creep away before closing time

to forage in the skip out back
and the nervy confessionals staring
at their own reflections as they sip
blood-red liquor distilled from worn-out hearts.

Occasionally the place falls silent
when a pale figure in a black cape
and floppy hat loops in distractedly.
Ah, the real thing, they mutter enviously

but all in all, nothing much happens here
and it can get messy as the evening wears on.
The poems grow ever more edgy, you see,
dreading the thought of another lonely night unread.

Poems About Death, Poems About Sex

It was funny, we were all laughing
the day our English teacher lost the run of himself,

flung his book on the desk and walked out.
I'd say he was after having a row with the wife.

Last class before lunch,
and we were starving.

Did he think we would get all perky
over a boring old poem about death?

What's the big deal? Death is everywhere,
even in real life.

I should know, there's a graveyard near our house,
I can see the headstones from my bedroom window.

When I was younger I often stayed up watching for ghosts,
never spotted any real ones down there, not even on Halloween.

Dad used to tell the old joke
about people 'dying to get in there'

but that was before the country went belly-up
and he lost his job. These days he is mostly in daze mode.

No jokes, he barely talks at all,
not even to Mom who seems cross all the time.

When the teacher came back I put up my hand:
Are there any better poems, Sir? These are real boring.

He started naming poets as if he was listing makes of cars:
Ferrari, Porsche, Lamborghini. Just showing off.

When I got home I went to my room,
the one that looks down on the graveyard,

googled 'poems about sex' and sure enough,
pages of sexy poetry to choose from.

I thought about bringing a few into class,
but in the end I didn't,

it would probably have caused trouble
and Mom has enough on her plate just now.

The Pool

Sometime in the afternoon
I heard the squabble of pheasants in the woods

then something splashed in the pool behind my back.
I had been watching for a long time,

no shadow-flicker, no movement,
nothing only the smooth grey stillness

and the tiny v shapes
behind the scurrying water beetles.

The moment I turned it came, one single plop,
then all was calm once more,

the gentle ripples spreading from a fading epicentre.
I waited all evening, never lifting my gaze

but the pool kept its secret.
Now I will never know.

Mason As Artist

Granite would break your heart,
hard as the hobs in the main hall of the Devil,
and no amount of cursing or coaxing will work,

not even the threat of the crusher
and the shame of being spread
beneath the surface of a road.

Try dressing a face on those mule-thick lumps
and you will earn your shilling.
Don't worry, I'll put manners on them for you.

A broad pitching-chisel with a fresh tungsten edge
and an eye in your head for the vein,
the only weapons to frighten those awkward boyos.

You could be pinging away all day,
might as well be scratching a wet match
unless you have the tungsten and the eye.

Spend an hour here with me in the morning
and you'll learn something
about the nature of quarry-run granite.

Pure solid spite, bad-minded,
it knows what to do alright
but will always refuse to oblige.

The Wilde Poems

1. Sir William Wilde at Moytura House

(Cong, Co Mayo 1865)

I

There he goes,
galloping the roads in his fancy phaeton
with the big painted wheels,
hemp rope for reins as if he was a turf-man.

What takes him every day
to the old fairy-forts I wonder?
Measuring and stepping, uprooting rocks
that have stood here since Noah.

There's no luck in that carry-on,
the 'little people' like to hold their secrets close.
He will meet the black hag some night on the road,
feel her cold breath on his neck.

They say he took the bones of a giant
from the rock-pile at Ballykine,
packed them into a travelling bag
and away with him.

Nothing good will come of it,
that's for certain sure,
and if the curse does not land on him
it will light on those who will come after.

Surely a smart man the likes of him,
out in the broad world,
must know the misfortune
he is drawing down around his shoulders.

II

I heard the Firbolg host last night
as they passed westward through the fields
to face the long-dead Dannans.

Their spirit-shapes were seen
swirling in the mists off the Corrib.
The annals surely have it right.

This is the place where their warrior bones
have been resting under the piled cairns.
All must be recorded, all must be made known.

III

I am vilified in Dublin
where the street-singers mock my name:
If you will listen to tell I will try
How the oculist opened Moll Travers's eye.

She's mad of course,
no one believes her,
but every tongue wagging.
A farthing she got in the end for her troubles.

I tried to wash my hands of her, oh yes!
Twice the infernal lady went to Liverpool
but returned, demanding more,
ranting through the city.

The lawyers have stuffed their pockets,
the rogues, but let that be an end to it.
I thought to find peace here in the West
where at least the peasants salute me on the road.

Surely they have heard something of the case.
My Lady wife arrives next week
and the boys will soon be down
from school for the summer.

Ah, the boys! How they love Moytura.
The teachers all sing their praises.
I have high hopes,
high hopes indeed.

2. More Lives Than One

I

See him step from the hansom,
resplendent in his long coat
with its black velvet collar
and green carnation buttonhole.

The scented theatre is throbbing,
the dazzling wit.
Author! Author!
The sheer genius of the man.

II

Handcuffed and in convict stripes,
he waits at Clapham Junction
for the Reading train

on the open platform with his prison guards
in grey November drizzle
amid the afternoon bustle.

Strangers point at the grotesque,
humbled and distressed,
then someone calls his name.

A jeering mob gathers.
He bows a close-cropped head,
with his shoulder wipes spittle from his cheek.

Every day for one full year
he weeps at that same hour
and for the exact same space of time.

III

In Naples there is a lonely garden
where the burdened find release
when their load becomes too weighty.

One starless night a stooping man
came to that shady place
to sit alone in his great despair.

He heard a rustling noise,
then misty, cloud-like things appeared.
He knew they were the restless spirits

of those who had gone before
but had found no peace. He left the park
and trudged the hill to face another day.

3. 'No Red Rose In All My Garden!'

'The Nightingale and The Rose'- Oscar Wilde

Sleep an impossibility
behind the 'dripping wall',
he takes his mind away

to the great purple mountains
where their hunting lodge stood
on the edge of a rushy lake

full of melancholy carp that never moved
unless roused by ancient songs
and local boatmen's whisperings.

A green Connemara hillock climbs from the mists,
ribbed with lazybeds from famine days.
The grave of a selfish giant who refused to share.

He hears his mother's voice
reading Aeschylus as she paces the floor
in their Dublin mansion on the genteel Square

with its beautiful gardens safely locked
behind spiked railings.
Only those with the key may enter.

Then dawn at last creeps over Reading
where even the dandelions refuse to show their faces.
Ah, on what little things does happiness depend!

4. Wilde At Berneval-Sur-Mer

After the singing,
the strawberries,
the last raised glass

he takes the lamp and climbs
to the attic room of his misery,
removes his Wanderer's mask.

In the mirror, a loathsome face,
hideous, it must be destroyed.
But first a valediction,

how each man kills the thing he loves.
For ghostly Melmoth, whose name he has stolen,
no swift dagger-slash,

his will be a slower wounding,
shambling through the boulevards,
but certain death nonetheless.

5. Oscar Wilde's Last Absinthe

Look how he comes,
shuffling from Dupoirier's place
like a man dragging the spars of his cross.

The English say he is a monster,
an ogre of strange desires,
how little they know in England.

The most generous of men,
at least when his pockets are full.
They say he drank with the Prince of Wales.

He likes to sit here in the afternoon
sipping his absinthe, away from the boulevards
where they leave when he enters.

What a life of thorns.
He is welcome in my café anytime.
Ah! Monsieur Melmoth, bonsoir...

Picker

He lifts the lid,
unspools the wool-woven strap,

next the instrument itself,
gently raised from its nest as if sound asleep,

all the while caressing its polished neck,
the curved veneer of its ribs and flanks.

He eases a plectrum onto his thumb,
picks a few tentative notes,

fingers scurrying across the frets
like night-mice over sleepers

in some far-forgotten railway station.
Then he is up and running,

gaining speed,
pulling away hot and raw,

and we are his passengers
and we all understand.

Lilter

No instrument ever mastered
not even the penny whistle.

Where would he have found time
for such 'nonsense' as a lad?

The barrow, the spade, splitting stones
with a loose-handled sledge.

Bits of tunes tipped in a ramshackle henhouse
tucked behind the shadow-gable of his mind.

The boat to England. Lurking, pint in hand,
on the edge of a Saturday night 'session'

or listening, ear tilted,
to a balladeer or fiddler,

through the drink-drenched wistfulness
of late night lock-ins.

Silent, until that wet day at tea-break in the site hut,
the gangerman absent,

he lilted a tune for the lads from home
ranged about on planks and cement bags,

a note-perfect jig skittering off his tongue,
surprising all, including himself.

They danced in their overalls and lead-heavy boots,
yelping and linking elbows, rising bomb-clouds of dry cement,

and he on an upturned bucket, lilting and clapping,
his hunched shoulders bouncing in time

until stifled at last by the swirling dust and the laughter
he made for the door

spread his new wings,
cock-crowed and was free.

Gospel

He strokes the keyboard,
long chords swelling
like spring tide by the quay.

The choir and congregation swing,
filling the room with praise
and high-five happiness.

But something about his side-smile,
the shake of his long grey mane,
the red feather pinned to the side of that black felt hat

hanging nonchalantly on the back of his chair
says he would be more at ease down town
in a place with a cool name like Saxo's or Luke's Joint

sipping bourbon and playing the blues
while a curvy lady in a leopardskin dress
smiles at him angelically from the bar.

Soon The Deep Stars

Sunset folds behind the island
like the hem of your red dress.

Soon the deep stars will come to mingle
with the strollers on the esplanade

and I will be a gospel choir
from somewhere south, the full ensemble,

and you will be the swaying conductor,
your curvetting baton keeping time,

leaning in, holding the tremolo,
building to the final chorus,

that extended *hummm*,
a great roll of the eyes,

the long and glorious
oohh yeah!

The Village-Women Keen
for the Fiddler

You are in the silent country now
and the way the notes would fly from your bow
to fall on our toes like sparks from an anvil

but we will wake you well, Fiddler Jimmy,
then settle you comfortable
in a snug box of the finest timber.

There is a soft bed waiting on the south slope
to catch the morning sun and the first trumpet blast.
It is only what you deserve

having never said no to a neighbour.
How you could handle a spade
and that bursting garden behind the house.

Where are you tonight Fiddler Jimmy?
Richer they would have us believe,
no more fear of darkness or the winter gales.

You will not be left alone
in the dark hours before the clay,
you can depend on that,

and tomorrow
we will carry you
the long way around.

Starlings in October

After the showers
the starlings appear above the reeds,
wing to the east then back again on a single whim,

swooping low across the marshland
towards the hillock where cattle stand and gaze
at the spectacle. They circle, climb,

dip to the west in one great sweep,
shapeshifting against the October sky
like a concertina squeezed and drawn

by a woman years ago in a West Clare cottage,
fingers lively then, the tunes reeling
over the flagstoned floor

and across the fields to a neighbour's yard
where a young man cocks his ear and dreams
of a day she will play for him

in the evening when his day's work is done
and they can watch the starlings dance
in the high arc of their exuberance.

Adult Education

Someone mentions a post-reception party
but you know only too well the way of it.

Dawn will find you shivering in the foetal position
beneath a flimsy duvet,

nibbling the corner of an eviscerated pillow
bunched in the shape of a terrifying, conch-like ear

in somebody's mouldy bedroom,
with an unsettling stain you hope is wine

splashed like the map of Indonesia
across the grey ceiling just above your head.

All Soul's Day

The day appears at the end of the street
shaven-headed and trembling,

as if turned from the night-shelter
to scrounge through the town

while darkness watches from the bare wood
shifting between the dripping trees

and rotting undergrowth, restless,
biding its time.

Galway Haiku

Green steeple and dome,
Spring and the tumbling river
mist-kissing Long Walk.

Tribetown

Days when the soft mists wait off shore
and the sun arrives to fill this place with jigs and reels
drawing the chill from the old limestone,

youth sprawls in tribal circles
with banjos, drums and didgeridoos,
strange rhythms picked up on walkabout.

Here the world finds space to draw its breath,
and the truce holds, while the river
tumbles by like a Macnas parade.

In the Square the sculpted sails
hold steady, frozen in their hooker's curve,
and nobody is waiting for the spell to break.

Crossing Eyre Square

When you see a young couple,
no more than kids really,
crossing Eyre Square with backpacks,

she, a waif, clinging to his lanky arm,
as if he was the one
who knew where they were going,

or that shaggy busker,
younger than your own son,
stringing a banjo on the steps by the fountain,

you cannot help but fix a stony face, almost paternal,
to match that grand hotel, set there like a magistrate,
to scowl on a world no longer battened down.

Midmorning and a shrieking hoard of long-limbed babes
dash by, still abuzz from the nightshift on the town,
dragging hand-luggage towards the station.

Clearly, you mutter, these are the final days,
this dismantled world is hanging by a thread,
just hanging now by a thread…And yet!…

It can't be that you hanker for those railed-off times,
the servant and the served, the polished pulpit,
the haughty landlord on his limestone plinth?

Surely not, and there was more if you remember –
the chaste fumblings in shadows by a gate,
the guilt-filled weeks, the rantings on eternal fires of hell.

There's been enough of that.
No! Let the revellers come to sprawl upon the grass,
to kiss in sunlight,

to feast and dance the jigs and reels of love
in wild sean-nós style
and maybe chase some demons from their earthly hells

where they held sway behind high walls
while we passed by, our eyes downcast,
in case we might see smoke.

At Gregory's Sound

Where the cliffs fall to the shore at Gregory's Sound
there is a desolate wilderness
of boulders and shale,
the islanders call it the Vale of Tears.

It was here the people gathered
whenever the ship out from Galway took shelter,
waiting for the gales to shift
before crossing for the New World.

They would cry out the names of their loved ones,
waked and embraced for the last time only days before,
then wait for the tattered replies
to come ashore on the wind

and sometimes, if the rains lifted,
they might glimpse faint shapes
in familiar clothes waving
from the rolling deck.

Fishermen churning by this lonely spot
well know what they see glistening
on the grassy mounds among the rocks
is not always the morning dew.

The Way Things Happen

I had a life once you know,
not much
but not this.

It's the creeping way things happen;
the tide miles out and the next thing you know
it's back and nibbling your toes.

I used to go to all the funerals in the Abby,
passed the day, sometimes people shook my hand,
told me they were sorry for my troubles.

A priest noticed me,
said I could come in and sit by the radiator,
on cold days anyway.

I used to stay over in the corner
where they light the candles to St. Anthony,
(St. Jude would be more in my line).

It worked out well for a while,
then he saw the coin-box,
noticed the lock had been forced.

Sea-Stallion

Too old now for the open boat
on frothy days anyway,
we thought to go back as far as Na Clocha,

Steve and myself, and drop a line,
maybe try for some rockfish hiding
in the cracks at the foot of the cliff.

The tide was big that morning with a good gust up,
so we sat back on a stone
to see what the day would do.

Steve saw it first, rising far out,
its straining head and neck, a flowing white mane,
its huge chest, its great round flanks

and a white tail curling high behind
as it charged headlong towards the shore.
We knew straight away it was the sea-stallion.

Nearing the cliffs he rose on his hind legs
and with one mighty leap cleared the face,
clattering down on the flag

not twenty steps from where we stood
making the sign of the cross,
for what we had seen was not of this world.

He steadied himself and headed off across the island.
Not a word did we say to anyone,
who would have believed us anyway at our age?

But when Paddy Dick found his mare to be with foal
and couldn't explain it, we spoke up. I've not been over
to the cliffs since and my sleep is often astray.

Departure

(Shannon Airport, January 2013)

We catch sight of him again
behind the window at Departures,

that familiar looping saunter.
He turns to wave,

smiles at our thumbs-up gestures.
You squeeze my hand,

as hard as you did
that night of his birth,

and he is gone.

An Old Man Remembers
His Daughter

His arms across the bog are two magpie wings,
his feet are hollowed log-boats
deep-sunk in a turf-bank,

this man whose chest is a frozen tarn
in a pitch-dark valley of night-echoes
miles from where the last road turns back

towards the laughing-town
where she went that time
to get away once and for all

from the silence and the squelch of wintry sky.
Sometimes he thinks she might come back tomorrow,
or the day after tomorrow.

World News

With the rain tapping the window,
the heat not yet turned on,
I stretched out on the bed

in a small-town hotel room
and watched the long caravan of world strife
endlessly scrolling across the t.v. screen.

Later, with no let-up in the weather or the grim news,
I made my way across the road
to a welcoming pub with a blazing fire

where a local at the counter told me
he rarely left the parish, hadn't been to the city in years.
'They'd slit your throat for a farthing up there.

Down here the Kilmallock crowd
have always been very clannish
and the Bruff crowd are no better,

anyone would tell you that,
so where could a man go?'
I told him he had it all said.

Night-Callers

I came here straight from the hospital,
haven't been back since, can't face it.
It's alright but full of old crocks.
I'm one now myself, I suppose.

The surgeon tried his best but the fingers never came right,
their lump-hammer did the damage.
I can handle a spoon but not a cup
and the knife and fork bests me.

I'll manage, but grace of God that Maura wasn't alive,
the way she kept everything so nice
and all her dishes lined up on the dresser.
No, I could never darken that door again.

The Sergeant calls in sometimes if he's passing,
brings me a little drop,
stays for a chat if he has the time,
tells me the night-callers are still at it.

Crash

For a while we stood around
like ballroom dancers in a power cut

or kids in a school playground,
their ball having smashed the Head's window,

unsure of our next move,
hands covering our gaping mouths.

Late in the Day

We were leaning on our shovels waiting for concrete
when a jeep swung in at the gate,

raced down the cratered track past the topsoil mound,
empty tar-barrels flying like depth charges,

slid to a halt outside the makeshift office,
spraying the flimsy site-hut with a fantail of gravel.

The two rickety steps conquered in a single bound,
bareknuckling dents into the hastily bolted door.

The foreman came running from behind the tool-shed,
hands waving in the air.

Our visitor lifted a concrete block,
I want what's mine,

heaved it through the office window
then tore back up the site and out the gap.

Mattie looked at me, then at the sky:
It's getting a bit late in the day for concrete now.

The long shadow of the crane fell skeletal
across the waterlogged drains.

Darkness already bundling in the grey house-shells,
some roofed, others roofless,

and a picture in our old school book came into my mind,
history I suppose, an abandoned famine-village,

mud-cabins collapsing,
the people swallowed up.

Tipoff

I saw him as we crossed to Arrivals,
trousers arse-sagging,
barking into a mobile lost in a furry paw,

white shirt pot-bellied loose,
sweat stained, crumpled,
obviously one of our own.

Save the new four-wheel trailer anyway Jack,
hitch it to the jeep then out the gap.
If anyone asks, you know fuck all.

The bastards are on their way to padlock the site,
I got the tipoff a minute ago
and I getting off the plane.

Our eyes met, he shook his head,
the underdog's gesture
as the game slips away.

Why is it always uphill and against the wind?
And I too willed Jack to get moving,
faster than he had ever moved before.

When the Leaves Start to Tremble

The late night movie was about a railroad magnate
who paid gunslingers to drive the homesteaders
from their little farms. The sheriff, a decent man,
was shot in the back. I fell asleep before the end
but it wasn't looking too good for the farmers.

Next day an expert on the radio,
voice smooth as a crystal ball,
was discussing the country's woes.
I'd say he would have been on the side
of the railroad magnate.

The world has been staring at me for a good many years
through that dusty windowpane;
the leaves on those ash-trees around the house
start to tremble just before they decide it is time to fall.
I locked the gate and whistled for the dogs to come inside.

City of Babel

An evening boatman poles by, his back
to the crumbling towers of failed arrogance.

Even the herders with their goats will not shelter
in this accursed place of dust and silence,

where the roped spars and seized pulleys
swing idle in the red winds.

Underworld

I move the big terracotta flowerpot
and find myself towering above
a shanty-town of crawlies and creepies,
their frail withered-leaf houses, their muddy main-streets.

The urge is to stomp but what, I wonder,
must life be like in their dank village?
It takes the woodlice a long time to sense the danger,
unlike the wriggling centipede who sidles off

like a dealer fleeing a drug-squad swoop
or that shiny devil-beetle,
all bling and pimpy attitude,
hightailing it for the suburbs around the corner.

That fat woodlouse is obviously a dawdling fellow,
like an ageing blues-player slow-ambling for the underground,
hunched and weary from years spent busking
and forced now to move along once again.

He must face home this evening
empty handed to his wife
who will accuse him of slipping back
into old habits, liquor and the numbers game.

A loner in a flat grey cap, he has no greeting
for the stocky emigrant women-woodlice
with their black shawls wrapped high,
who are wandering about aimlessly now,

bewildered by the sudden splash of warm sunlight
which reminds them of the old country,
vines and donkeys and each day
the same as the one before.

It is fair to assume that the little community
will settle back into something like their old routine
once the pot has been replaced. The god-fearing
will cling to the belief that their prayers were answered.

In time, the survivors will recall this terrible day
and try to advise the young woodlice about catastrophes
but the youth will roll their carefree bug-eyes,
flick their antennae in that casual manner

so infuriating to their elders
and mutter among themselves about their parents
who cannot relax and keep behaving as if
the roof over their heads could just one day disappear.

The Druid's Wife Speaks
Against The Saint

His bent staff will never sprout shoots.
We have the spirit of the yew
and the mystery in the drooping willow.

At my husband's glance the river flows uphill,
the starlings sky-dance
above the King's high Dún.

This puny reprobate in tattered sandals
turning men against their wives, wives against their men,
will not succeed.

The great fire must burn.
Leave us to our ways, I say,
they have served us well enough.

Reunion

Pre-dinner drinks, black-tie smiles,
pumpkin soup, guinea fowl and silver spoons.
Another toast and the port goes around again.

Old vellum creaking
on hidebound memories,
a shirt-button slipped at the neck.

Radicals now, romantics even.
Tomorrow a canter on the thoroughbred,
born to ride the high saddle.

Death of a Poet

i.m. Seamus Heaney

So this is how the news arrives,
a colleague's quiet knock on a classroom door,
the beep-beep of a daughter's text,
the corridor empty and silent
then the bell knelling classes to a close.

In the Hills Above Argostoli

Five thousand soldiers died that day,
in the hills above Argostoli.
Italian, of the Acqui Division,

riddled where they stood disarmed,
some praying, others crying,
the names of wives, mothers, children on their tongues.

Desperate acts of futile companionship,
heroes, cowards, brave or bewildered,
staring at the indifferent muzzles,

one youth forced to sing,
he was known for his voice
in the taverns of Kefalonia.

They called on the wounded
to come from the mound of death for help
then shot them where they crawled.

We were on our way to Sami
and the ferry for Ithaca in our little rented car
when we came upon the place by chance,

a stone-paved monument
near a little copse of wild olive trees
by the side of a mountain road.

The sun not yet high and blazing,
we stood in that terror-stained spot,
afraid we might catch some faint age-echo

rising through the crusted soil
from the hellpit of deepest Tartarus,
listening instead to the pleasant strum of insects

and morning birdsong out of that ancient grove,
as heard by returning Odysseus
when he strode this path towards Penelope and home.

Hillwalker

At last the morning drizzles lift,
low November clouds
open like stage-drapes

and a sudden sun-splash
teems over Mweelrea,
brimming the deep pit

of its purple-dark corrie
with luminous winter light,
golden, almost glorious.

Eyes already scaling the high ridge,
bearings taken, the route figured out,
he swings his legs from the driver's seat,

laces brand new walking boots,
zips the rainproof jacket.
Game on.

He crosses the boggy foothills,
climbs the narrow path to the bare granite ledge.
If the day stays clear he will get his reward

high above the Black Lake, the Valley stretching south
to Killary, north all the way to Clew Bay
with nothing between him and the high heavens.

Afternoon and the thick Atlantic mists return.
Nightfall. The mountain hunches its shoulders,
draws a cowl over its stony bald head.

(ii)

She begins to wonder,
busies herself with the children's bath-time.

Sleep now and be good,
Daddy will talk to you in the morning.

His mobile unresponsive,
strange, he always calls if he's late?

She dozes, night-hours dripping silence,
wakes with a start and knows.

Triptych: The Bridge

(i)

He will drown again tomorrow evening
and every evening
for the remainder of the run
in the theatre we have just left.

An old man's life ending by consent
under the cold waters of Chesapeake Bay,
his wife and son watching
helplessly from the shore.

The insurance money will see them right
according to the simple plot.
Sad, I had grown fond of him
in 'the two hour's traffic of our stage'.

(ii)

We cross the bridge to the carpark.
Up ahead the cathedral stony-faced and haughty,
the river swollen from recent downpours,
all curling swallow-holes and frothy through the arches.

At times the city's wounded find their way here,
place their palms flat on the parapet and vault.
We see their ghostly faces peering from makeshift posters,
photocopied and hastily stuck on poles around the town.

I think of grey-hooded Charon gleefully watching from his boat
as he poles through the reeds of swampy Acheron
to collect the newly dead who have gathered on the bank.
Who would go there willingly?

But what do I know of the dark hours
or the darker rains, the vast tundra without shelter?
The wipers clear the windscreen, the car grows cosy,
you squeeze my hand, soon we will be home.

    (iii)

I'm not familiar with the exact details.
We heard the big Sikorsky hovering above the river's open mouth.
When I meet his broken father I don't know what to say.

Usually daft things: *He wouldn't be too happy*
with United's performance this weather.
A grand young-lad, never passed without saying hello!

Friends still leave messages
on his Facebook page,
how mad is that?

Cemetery Sunday

Whatever it is the dead know
you know now Mother,
and I doubt it's what you imagined.

Best not go there,
and anyway, Mother,
I don't want an argument.

So we wire-brush the headstone,
scrape away the yellow lichen from
the two names - James and his wife Kathleen.

I try not to think about those reposing
all about in their carefully chosen garments,
the good suit seldom worn,

the favourite blouse, a rosary entwined,
cheeks, throats, hips, pelves, shankbones,
wrapped in the harsh canvass of Rahoon's stony clay.

We plant a few more flowers,
all nice for Cemetry Sunday
and begin to feel the afternoon's damp chill.

I once asked a priest at a wedding reception
what it was he thought the dead felt.
He stared at me as he swirled his whisky.

A lot less than we do ourselves, I'd imagine.
At least he was trying to be honest,
or maybe it was only the drink.

Navy-Blue Suit

A cheerful man, a family man everybody said,
a game of darts and a fiver each way on Saturdays.

His widow eventually got his few things out of the locker
at the depot where for years he covered the early shift.

A young one behind the desk with purple nails
in a navy-blue suit was supposed to help with the paperwork.

She never forgot the nails and the black stripes
on that young one's navy-blue suit.

Cormorant at the Mouth
of the Corrib

She has been standing all night
by the curtain in a third-floor hotel room.

Oldtown empty and rain-rinsed.
Black-wet rooftops, the tumbling river,

the cold stone harbour, the bay.
Gulls, frantic for their dawn morsel.

No passing straggler has glanced at her window,
no one she knows will come to the door.

On the unused bed her open diary,
like a dead bird wing-spread by the pillow.

Near the bridge a cormorant, jet-slimy,
eyes the sliding current, patient but alert.

At last the snake-necked dive, silent and traceless,
like a dress slipping from the shoulders,

a wound miraculously healing
after the laying on of blessed hands.

On Reading 'Birthday Letters'

You try not to hear their night-ravings,
but the walls are so thin.
Soon you know all about his 'roving eye'
her 'problems with family'.

They can be seen going in and out,
a big loping Geordie with books or a fishing rod,
and a blonde Bostonian with a pram
trying hard to be a Yorkshireman's wife.

Before long you are spying from the upstairs window
as she weeds the poppy-bed in her red skirts
or paints the old beehive in the far corner
while he instructs from a distance.

You grow ever more concerned,
the raised voices, the long silences.
Perhaps you should call around, introduce yourself,
but there is an invisible 'keep out' sign.

Jumpy now at the sound of distant sirens,
something you find difficult to explain.
It's been very quiet for days.
Was that somebody coughing?

Now That I Have Reached A Certain Age

the remaining hours of my life
break cover with increasing regularity
to gather beneath my window,
shuffling about in a derisive manner,
before racing like scavengers
towards the horizon
with the occasional backward glance,
their sly snouts to the ground,
sharp teeth bared
in vicious and vindictive grins.

Afterlife

There is nothing I wish to say this evening
except perhaps to tell you straight up
how awkward things will be in the afterlife
should we meet there by chance at some celestial gathering

where you will expect me to comment
on the elegance of your wings
and the brilliance of your snow-white robe
as you keep vigil over my shoulder

for the arrival of recently deceased celebrities,
all the while complaining loudly
about the dreadful harp music
and the quality of the nectar.

Should you bother to enquire where I have been lurking
since my arrival eons ago
I will tell you that it is over between us,
citing your lifelong practice of making me feel dumb,

how you constantly took the opposite view
and enjoyed telling cruel anecdotes with me as the fall-guy:
the plant I couldn't name, the book I hadn't read,
the composer whose aria I could not indentify.

For this is the life I presently accept,
your lofty bemusement, my fumbling uncertainty,
which is why I will not, after all, be mentioning tonight
my plan to spend all of eternity avoiding you.

Such thoughts I have learned to keep to myself,
to savour on those long and silent drives home.

Thoughts at Thirty Thousand Feet

Settling back at thirty thousand feet
I couldn't help but wonder what the ancients,

for whom flight was the domain of the immortals,
would have made of EI 137 Shannon to Boston.

As we climbed above Galway Bay
it occurred to me

that the day will inevitably arrive
when Death's winged messenger

will break through the puffball clouds just about here
with a flap of unearthly feathers to be greeted

by this exact vista, the islands, the great Connemara
mountains and my home town there to the east.

He will following the coast
towards the suburbs

looking for a house with roof-windows
and an untidy garden.

A balding man will be found on his patio
enjoying the sunshine and maybe a nice pot of afternoon tea,

pen and notepad on the table
with some lines crossed out.

The man will be wondering
why the afternoon has suddenly turned chilly,

if he should take something
for the nagging indigestion

and the strange tingling in his left arm
that has definitely been intensifying since lunchtime.

Ultrasound

for Eoghan

(i)

A peaceful face in a bell suit,
iconic helmet, life-giving hose,

like a black and white still
from an old movie about deep-sea-diving,

and there, yes, little fingers,
all buoyant in a maternal ocean,

and floating now on the sideboard
among the other family faces,

some gone, others growing,
mystifying, tiny, immense.

(ii)

It's been more than an hour
since we waved our friends away in a taxi

and here we are, still lingering at the kitchen table
over a second bottle of Chianti,

humming along to the dishwasher as it croons
something smoochy to itself,

about the 'marketplace in old Algiers',
if I'm not mistaken.

(Did I mention the ultrasound printout
propped on the shelf – a first grandchild?)

And now the mood is such
that if a stranger appeared at the patio door

with a blunt instrument and wearing a ski-mask
I would wave amiably, point to the bottle

then to the cupboard where the good crystal goblets
are stored and invite him to join us in a toast

once the orchestra in the dishwasher
has come safely to rest.

The Rest is Silence

We joke of cosy lead-lined coffins built for two,
an Aladdin's lamp to hold our blended ashes,

elaborate arrangements for death as for sex
to please our flesh and maybe our bones,

but there is no real consolation,
that is the truth at the empty hollow of it.

Soon after lovemaking the vague fear returns,
not of death but of being left behind,

it can be felt
burrowing like a taproot

through rain-soaked clay
to touch the varnished lid.

GERARD HANBERRY is an award-winning poet living and working in Galway on the west coast of Ireland. This is his fourth book of poems and follows on his 2009 collection *At Grattan Road,* also from Salmon Poetry, a collection the *Irish Times* said was 'bursting at the seams with fine poems'. Gerard Hanberry has also published a biography of the Wilde family *More Lives Than One — the Remarkable Wilde Family Through the Generations* (The Collins Press). He is a teacher of English at St. Enda's College, Galway and delivers a creative writing module at the National University of Ireland, Galway. He lives, overlooking Galway Bay, with his wife Kerry.